Praise for *Bodymap*

"These poems bring love to moments that usually slip out of conversations, and get lost in our general hustle to prove that we are human. These poems are a gift for your love for self, your love itself and everyone you love. It is rare that a poet priestess offers words that allow us to emerge reborn with dirt, glitter and tenderness. This is one of those opportunities. Revere it. Revel in it. Read it again and again!"
—ALEXIS PAULINE GUMBS, author, creator, *Eternal Summer of the Black Feminist Mind*

"*Bodymap* uses the alchemy of the voice on the page to transform words into an ache in the pit of me. I want what these poems demand: to be free to love & die, to be resurrected in time, & to be restored by desire. Piepzna-Samarasinha has located where this body houses the smirk learned from the sidewalk, the reason to do the difficult, and the blessings for the best worst thing. Rereading is not an option, it's a requisite."
—MEG DAY, author, *Last Psalm at Sea Level*

"These poems carry numerous bloodlines; ancestors, lovers, chosen survivor families and remembered lives. Sharp, yet remarkably compassionate, Piepzna-Samarasinha knows that the poem is no place for tidy inquiry and easy answers. She offers her own tenacious guts and veins on each and every page. Only someone who understands rage and reconciliation and blood and bone can write like this."
—AMBER DAWN, author, *How Poetry Saved My Life: A Hustler's Memoir* and *Sub Rosa*

"Leah's side eye can cut you, but her maps to working-class, disabled, queer Asian home-girl medicine might also save your life. At the locus of social justice, documenting survival, and the joy of sex, here are love poems to Hondas and cedar plank shacks and fucking in places where we are hated. Leah is working and working it. Hurt is here, but so is survival, and all the joy and mascara-running beauty it affords."

—BAO PHI, author, *Sông I Sing*

"Leah Lakshmi Piepzna-Samarasinha's *Bodymap*, is a cartographer's worst nightmare. In navigating through this gorgeous and complicated terrain of pages, we find ourselves amidst a landscape that refuses to be charted by the voyeur's gaze--a landscape that is defined by its own muscle memory, by the reclamation of its own shifting form, and by honouring the exquisite labour of its own heaving chest."

—ANNAH ANTI PALINDROME

Bodymap

POEMS

Leah Lakshmi Piepzna-Samarasinha

Mawenzi House

©2015 Leah Lakshmi Piepzna-Samarasinha

Except for purposes of review, no part of this book may be reproduced in any form without prior permission of the publisher.

We acknowledge the support of the Canada Council for the Arts for our publishing program. We also acknowledge support from the Government of Ontario through the Ontario Arts Council.

We acknowledge the financial support of the Government of Canada through the Canada Book Fund for our publishing activities.

 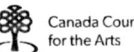 

Cover art: *Assimilation* by Texta Queen
Author photo: Naty Tremblay
Cover design: Jaaron Collins

Library and Archives Canada Cataloguing in Publication

Piepzna-Samarasinha, Leah Lakshmi, 1975-, author
    Bodymap / Leah Lakshmi Piepzna-Samarasinha.

Poems.
ISBN 978-1-927494-50-9 (pbk.)

    I. Title.

PS8631.I46B63 2015   C811'.6   C2015-900868-9

Printed and bound in Canada by Coach House Printing

Mawenzi House Publishers Ltd.
P. O. Box 6996, Station A
Toronto, Ontario M5W 1X7
Canada

www.mawenzihouse.com

For my lovers,
for my kid,
for my family on Sick and Disabled Queers

We use each other's raw bodies to remind ourselves how to pray.
—Amber Dawn

thanks and acknowledgements:

This book was written on unceded and occupied Mississauga of New Credit/ Three Fires Confederacy, Wiyot, Ohlone and Miwok land.

Thank you to Annah Anti-Palindrome and Vanessa Rochelle Lewis for creating Culture Fuck, where early versions of many of these poems were crafted, performed, and crafted again.

Aaron Ambrose's precise/quirked eyebrow, Hari Alluri's witty notes and k. ulanday barrett's "son! this is lushness!" editorial eyes burned this manuscript better. I also thank Meg Day for finding time during the tightest schedule to offer notes, and for pointing out that I used the word "corset" a lot.

For so much collective genius, care, lovework and inspiration, thank you to my hearts: Chanelle Gallant, Arti Mehta, Manish Vaidya, Maya Chinchilla, Cherry Galette, Melannie Gayle, Jonah Aline Daniel, Gabriel Teodros, Bao Phi, Sham-e-ali Nayeem, Victor Tobar, Aaron Ambrose, Hari Alluri, Meg Day, K. Ulanday Barrett, Annie Murphy, Luna Merbruja, Rosina Kazi, Lisa Amin, Liz Latty, Bruin Runyon, Beast Von Fancy, Stacey Milbern, Ryan Li Dahlstrom, Setareh Mohammad, Harsha Walia, Farrah Khan, Zavisha Chromicz, SB McKenna, Aruna Zehra Boodram, Loree Erickson, Lenny Olin, David Findlay, Nalo Hopkinson, Billie Rain, Zakiyah Iman Jackson, Gesig Isaac, Bilquis Bulbul, Qwo Li Driskill, Elokin Cheung, LeRoi Newbold, Naima Lowe, Amber Dawn, Fabian Romero, Micha Cardenas, Tre Vasquez, Walidah Imarisha, Alexis Pauline Gumbs, Stories of Queer Diaspora. All my Sacred Texts, Collective Dream writers. All the AMC fam, all the Sins Invalid fam, the Badass Visionary Healers, the Shark Pit, Casa Maize, every Mango. For Femmes of Colour: A Transnational Solidarity Group and Sick and Disabled Queers, Mixed/POC. Thank you for the Lambda. Thank you everyone who hired me to do something.

Gratitudes to my intuitive mentors, Vanissar Tarakali and Dori Midnight, for giving me advance degrees in how to listen.

Thanks to the MixedFemmeBroCave, where this book was completed in winter/spring 2014.

To the lovers who have transformed my life, deep bows. I stay grateful.

Some of these poems were published in *Bodymap*, a chapbook published in fall 2012.

Pieces in this book first appeared in the journals *Prism International, SAMAR, Jaggery, glittertongue, AS:US, Locked Horn, Nepatlera, 580 Split, Adrienne* and the anthology *Passage and Place*.

"Dirty River Girl" was commissioned and performed as part of Sins Invalid's 2009 performance, at Brava Theater, San Francisco, CA. "Crip Sex Moments" were created in collaboration with Ellery Russian, commissioned by Sins Invalid and performed at Theater Artaud, San Francisco, CA April 2011. "This is what I know about crazy" was written for *Breaking Code: The Intersections of Queerness and Madness,* curated by Blyth Barnow and Oscar Maynard for the 2014 National Queer Arts Festival.

The creation of *Bodymap* was supported by an Ontario Arts Council 2012 Writer's Reserve grant.

Contents

i. somewhere to run to

diaspora   2
my city is a hard femme   3

ii. evidence

bodymap   6
because sometimes, if you fuck me good, I will write you a poem   8
spoil me   9
a million dollars   11
every time I see you I think *what the hell was I thinking?*   13
evidence: anti-capitalist love poem 2012   15
love is resistance   16
good girl glosa   18
mulberries   20

iii. crip world

crip non haiku   22
love you like a 7 am healthy San Francisco free MRI   23
everyone thinks you're so lazy. don't let them   24
ode: crip cars   25
crip sex moments 1-10   26
dirty river girl   29
crip sex moments:
1. Cancel   35
2. Melanin night sky full of stars   37
3. Couch flirting   39
this is what I know about crazy   41
where I would find you   47
RSI   48

iv. hard girls

etymology of tough girl heart #2   50
I love hard girls   52
hussyflower   54
mash note   55
enough   56
because every brown girl needs/ where you find homegirl medicine   59
I will take care of you forever   63

v. wrong is not yours

insh'allah   66
wrong is not yours   68
airport ode #1   70
what it's like to be sri lankan in 2012 for those of you who aren't   72
how it happens   74
maestra teacher: a rebel teacher manifesta song in many parts.   75
the toronto ode suite:
1. *Dear Toronto: this, a love letter to you*   78
2 TSA: *we search bags randomly for the protection of the nation. today, yours was chosen*   80
3. *the immigrant suburbs*   82

vi. what kind of ancestor do you want to be?

My Father, Christmas 1991, As I Come Down the Stairs in Ripped Jeans and That Jane's Addiction T-Shirt With All the Naked People on It   84
when people ask me the last time i saw my mother   87
what kind of ancestor do you want to be?   88
sternum   91
what do you have?/ amulet   92
you know I'm gonna   94
nice brown parents   95
the day I decided to have you   96
the worst thing in the world   97

gratitudes

for the femmes. the krips. the crazies. the brokeass, the brown. the cleavage magic flies across borders. the plum. the protein. the honey blush sunsets. the land. the calling of the names for.

for the femmes. the improbable. the necklace of gem houses. for unlocked home doors. for the rest.

for the shared netflix login. the glitterfemme canes. the wheelchair pushers. the yellers. the nothing is too much. the split. the text message up all night crisis line.

for the redwoods, cedar and fir. for moonstone beach. for the white shark spawning ground.

for the perfect gf carrot coconut cake. the airmiles. the flower essences and gemstones. the backyard chickens and banana trees. the dancefloor kitchentable. the hustle. the break and the back and the back again.

for my lovers. for my friends. the beautiful ones in the ugly city. the uglybeautiful ones in the beautifulugly city.

for us.

i. somewhere to run to

diaspora
for k. ulanday barrett

to be in diaspora, maybe you are always a ghost
always missing something. your spirit hovers over bloor and
    lansdowne,
will hover over this bench on the berkeley library's second floor,
this alley in melbs, your grandparents' ashes memorial garden
you've flown to once:

    you are always looking over your shoulder. packing.
always panicking that this place won't
let you come back. border slam down, longing longing, over
shoulder, missing missing,
even when still here, about to go, gone—

perhaps the good in ghost
is that we everywhere we missing all the time:
you can call on my spirit that hovers bloor-and-lansdowne
I'll help you get the best score at the value village
get you your coffee served right, get you a cab, get you home
—the small miracles we survive on, so much less than we deserve.
your own ghost while you still alive, wishing and whispering you:
yes you came back, yes the the border will open,
you will live all the places your heart lives, you will come home.

my city is a hard femme

for Chanelle Gallant, after Qwo-Li Driskill's "nothing like a love poem for Greeley, Colorado/ Something like a Love Poem For Greeley Queers."

When I left Worcester, I took the smirk I learned from the sidewalk with me,
the girl gang of wild weed trees busting through every
vacant lot like a bank robbery
kicking down the door with the grin of getting everything for free.
I'm as hard-assed as every pretty broken thing in town,
every donut shop that'll tell you off in a heartbeat,
every dress with just one fucked-up thing
dug out of the Auburn TJ Maxxx quadruple clearance rack.
My city is a lovely tough girl
asking you what the fuck you're looking at,
all fitted up in skintight dirty redbrick & vinyl siding

My city a broken
                beautiful bitch with
a necklace of junk trees blooming
              from her throat.

ii. evidence

bodymap

For christmas, you write me your body.
For a love token, you offer me your body's map.
I stroke gold glitter finger tips and satin beige skin
on the crackle of paper unfolding.

Here, levitation.
There, a cock you created
out of your best imagination
that grows hard at a shot of cleavage
like straight-up amber whiskey.

In return, I gift you mine:
austere wordless infant
g spot shooting tears
ass stomp and razor blade switch
the pleasures and the dangers.

If a map is created by conquerers and the unconquered,
if the empire shrinks Africa but Africa remains how big she is,
these maps can be rewritten.
Rewrite my body.

Each day I tip tincture to lips,
drip three drips, whisper
change me.

If a map is an artifact made by explorers and colonizers
if a map names where bodies begin and end & who will own
their treasures

if a map can show the hideouts and secret passageways
the stashes of food and drugs and guns;

If we both have written maps to the stars
where our spirit flies out
and then written our return:
rewrite my body with me

you have wings tattooed on your breastbone
where I have the word *home* in cherry rust brown

I can already feel where we will make each other's bodies new

what story will we unfurl this time

change me

because sometimes, if you fuck me really good,
I will write you a poem

1. the whole love muscle car smells like hot cunt and dirty queer sex and burnt black dragon gloves scorched by my pussy. I don't know my own strength sometimes/I do/you do. You tell me *girl you could break me in half with those thighs*. In the backseat, half-empty 40-pound bags of millet and red lentils, my old house's wealth, my altar in a moving box, backup shoes and a femme time machine, my storage unit paperwork. In the front seat, you, murmuring, *huh, what do two awkward queers do?* murmuring pretty *cunt, pretty asshole, pretty.* between our legs and by the gearshift, speed, and a home on my chest and in my hands.

2. somebody's mama taught her baby boi the best workingclass manners. like ask others how they are doing often. tip your waitress 25 percent. be nice to folks doing shit jobs that you could be doing. and tell the girl you wanna fuck how pretty her ass is as she walks slightly ahead of you hipswish with her $2 cherry red slut thrift-store high heels.

3. you know us blue collar girls, we want product for our labour. meat in the seat. you know how to make the most out of 2.2 hours 2 pairs of knuckles and a borrowed bed.

spoil me

spoil me   survivor 3.0 sex   *are you 78% there?*   *you just left*
oh sweetie, you can tell? i think if you get on top of me I'll return
make my electromagnetic field hum
every hair rise up like wheat in a field
I'm making a memory   memory's already made   cast in small places
cedarshank shack roof tilted my bed and your breath and the shack rocking
your uproarious laughter and my cunt open and my wrack and my quiet child milk tender eye calm.
your breasts a surprise not a surprise
I want to be your girl   *it's been so long since*
i felt safe enough   *now I'm at 89%*
sweet pea I make a storm over your house
we wore the same colours same times
knew what the other was thinking first
poets but communication by colours and light was so much more elegant
you show up on time with fried chicken and collards you grew
you   your arms for me
gimme wings for you gimme home gimme light in body gimme this this light this particular
gimme this memory held held you

shouting
      you made me new, you made me new, you changed me, you changed me:

there are boy arms and girl breasts and a mouth that opens
& an infinity hovering

my skin knows how to talk in light vowels making a memory
    spoil me

a million dollars

I was pumping gas and you asked to pump it for some spare
   change.
I said sorry man, I have forty bucks to my name,
and you said, *well, you look like a million dollars*

& I wondered what a million dollars looks like
and what
minus 187 in overdraft plus fees looks like
cause I have looked like that.

I have looked like that
hard femme
don't fuck with me
switchblade ass swish
ima cut you at the bus stop for saying good morning
because I know everything that could and has come
from that moment

I have looked like
walking to the store in a miniskirt
after the car breaks and the phone breaks
and there is twenty dollars in a wallet
for the next two weeks

I'm a chipped manicure full of starry glitter
ends worn to the quick
from hard
hard work
I'm a gorgeous ass that's bedbound

I want you to love me messy in the morning
the same four year old booty shorts and no bra.
I want you to know
I beautiful
like a 36 year old on her couch
before the shower
the makeup
what I show you
what I will allow you to see.

I want you to love me
after the lipstick wears off.

every time I see you I think
what the hell was I thinking?

I wasn't thinking.
I was heart
broken. I was chest
cracked like axe. I was thinking
what the hell &
what's the worst thing
that could happen

the most dangerous questions
for any mean
broken-hipped
brown femme
who survived
whose pussy lips lift hopeful
twitch like touch me not petals
yearn for something worthy
of her open

white bois with eager butts
and nonprofit movement jobs you wanted
are just like whole foods take out:
when you are too tired
to cook your own food
you can pay too much
for a tasteless version of your culture
that promises it won't kill you.
afterwards, a greasy crunched compostable box
and debit charge so much more expensive
than you budgeted for.

a smear of your petals on the windshield
won't be the fought-for flavour
blooming on your tongue
your particular   vulnerable   longed for
homefood

evidence: anti-capitalist love poem 2012

I want it recorded
that once I lived in a little 7 x 14 foot cedar shack
with all its electricity through a heavy duty extension cord, and no lock,
in the back of a South Berkeley femme house
with black mold and four cats and nine roommates
kale, a fig tree, wild lilacs
I paid $175 a month
for a backyard hip deep in camellias, roses and magnolia,
for a hot tub that worked for a year before all of us and 12 friends a day broke it
(because everyone fucked in that hot tub),
for twenty bucks in the kitchen drawer for emergencies and 8 good shoulders.
I want it recorded that once I fucked you so good
that when you screamed the roof off the house
all the dogs in the neighborhood started to howl
and we both collapsed cracking up my fist inside you and my head on your breasts
as the corner baptist church bells pealed and pealed.
I want it noted that I made you come that open
that those dogs and bells howled,
that every moment passes and jewels.
I will enter into evidence that
I have made love to you in the front seat of your truck and my 1990 Chrysler New Yorker
both by wild California beaches
that there should be names for times in between the wars like this

that we grew up, we survived to have this
that we were rich.

love is resistance

driving over the blue winged bridge, you text me that you are
going to stinson beach
to camp out with a bunch of white people in a tidal pool.
I text back
*great, I am going to go help my youth not kill themselves due to
brandy and cece.*
I wonder if you will even know who I am talking about.
you text back: *good luck.* I text back: *love is resistance.*
you don't answer.
I drive over the blue winged bridge,
thinking of all the times I have heard the whispers of
kill yourself since I was 12
and how you have too,
and how here I am 37 and driving over this bridge
and haven't done it yet,
37 more years to go.

You didn't know when the dignity and resistance march was.
you came up behind me at the sink, wrapped fingers around belly
kissed my neck   brought me tea and oranges in bed,
shared your penicillin when we both had pneumonia
prayed before our first date
prayed every night for a while,
please god, don't let me fuck this up.

I accept all these in my body's archive
as a true story:
that you loved me that well
that I loved myself enough
to walk away when you stopped praying every morning

I drive across this bridge to love my youth hard
imagining their faces being like *why the fuck should I live*
if I go to jail for sewing scissors
if I go to heaven after being shot four times
for sitting in my car
My youth school me,
 all fourteen-year-old brace face
wearing a dress on the walk home for the first time.
We
have a check in where the prompt is
what way would you defend yourself
if you were attacked
We all choose violence
It's a choice.

Though at times every cell in my pissed-off
broke brown girl body wants to,
I choose not to set your gentrifying West Oakland house on fire
the bed where we made love
where you whispered
I want to experience the divine with you
and we did.

good girl glosa

We use each other's raw bodies to remind ourselves how to pray.
Queer grief is a blueprint. We got this shit wired tight.
Maybe we've become too good at losing? Are we trauma
bonded? I can't speak for the whole, only myself—
—Amber Dawn, "Queer Infinity Glosa"

Femme slut pretty pretty
baby sugar honey sweet
boo love boo face
cherry strawberry sweet thing
you—finally—the sweetest tart thing at the corner store,
and do you believe it?
All the honorifics cooed from a lover's full bulldog lower lip
Ass up is our best position
No one could have told us   we never would've believed
that someday we would kneel in this place, worshipped
We use each other's raw bodies to remind ourselves how to pray.

Where is this place our baby bodies sprinted towards
even when we were holding still for as long as possible?
Flight gave birth to birth. Fragment genius comes down to this
    heaven
of ass thwack, the miracle of taking it
the miracle of sweet good girl best girl good girl finally made it
made it home
We don't always know where this place is. We stumble
looking for the light switch, the exit sign.
Can we really just relax? When does this get pulled away?
Did we finally make it home?
Queer grief is a blueprint. We got this shit wired tight.

How does grief give birth to this place?
All the dandelion and calendula adaptogens in the crater of Nagasaki.
Your body, a small brown bottle of self heal and cosmos flowers which your lover said represent *the body's innate ability to heal itself*
and *all the parts coming together*
Gradually this became an adventure you got more sure cripfooted on the lover who rolled on top, kicked your guts wide, said *I want to rip you apart*
then shit, I got triggered, can you fuck yourself while I open your mouth up
and blow weed smoke in your face like a dirty uncle? Yes please
Maybe we've become too good at losing? Are we trauma?

But you weren't lost.
Did you finally get all of everything?
Did you finally stop losing?
I love you good girl best girl sugar babe gilded
laughing like all the bells of the iron bed jangling as you come your way home
We aren't lost
We are trauma
and these sweet sweet blossoms out the crater
We
bonded. I can't speak for the whole, only myself—
and we do, sugarblessed, our bodies do

mulberries

sometimes your hands are unexpectedly filled with the tenderest bleeding fruit. your love will see what they do not know is your favorite wild tree, they will break into a neighbour's front yard and climb her for you. fill your palms til they cup so much plum vulnerable breaking skin. you will not know you wanted someone to make you full like that. until that moment, when they do.

iii. crip world

crip non haiku

he said *you didn't seem like yourself that day*
I said *this is my self*
crunching my forehead to stay in the palace of words
Lamaze breathing through pain spikes
asking for a Vicodin with a shaking hand

love you like a 7 am healthy San Francisco free MRI

that loud   that terrifying
that held-on to hustled

that deep bell peeping and sounding your earth's shake
a magnet four times stronger than the earth's core

that's me sitting in a straight-backed chair in business casual
saying *yes, I'm his sister*   *yes, I'll stay in the room
during the procedure*

yelling at the tube they've stuck you in
*I know you can't hear me but I love you
and I'm saying it whether or not you can hear me*

everyone thinks you're so lazy. don't let them

this is your work:

slam the alarm over and over again.
then grab your Hitachi.
this will melt the shards of ice hardened in joints.
whole grains in tupperware, coffee and drugs await you.
do your yoga: your ancestors knew how to melt rock in hard times,
then get back home under the covers.

this is your commute:
to bless the daily act of breathing
as work as necessary as nine-to-five.

this your work:
like other invalids able to make art under the sheets
to be blessed just for breathing

this labour   not paid not union:
this is your work.
own it.
make sure you get paid what you are worth.
make sure you pay yourself first
make sure you say *work*
breathe *work*:
exhale and inhale:
our survival is
the opposite of lazy

ode: crip cars

for a decade, I live in cities
where nobody has a car
despite blizzards that close the Bergen subway stop
and *extreme cold warning, exposed skin will freeze in seven minutes*
and those sleeping-bag parkas you live in for six months straight
and—mostly—what I don't whisper:
bones that shiver and fall
that stare desperate at the disabled seat on the Ossington bus
but do not know how to insist.

how many times have I been slumping to the side,
weaving down the street, a hoochie with a cane
dodging the bus bench dudes hollering *you don't need that cane!*
cause I can carry you ma!
to fall out in your peeling velour embrace?
I can't stand up straight, remember my friend's name or how to
open a door
but I can shift into drive
and watch you inch up the 580 on ramp
and make it to school in 8 minutes not two hours on the 57.
Oh '92 honda accord station wagon
with no muffler to speak of and no shocks and no radio
with a broken triangle window that I gave up replacing
after the second time in two weeks—

oh crip car whose arms I fall into after thirty years on public transit
you are every other crip car some of us are lucky enough to have
carrying bones that ache and shiver out the house
to every doctor's appointment, play party, the bridge not the bus.
some people have a house at 38:
I have you.

crip sex moments 1-10

1. When sie slams me up against the wall at Ships in the Night and we both lose our balance and fall over (into x's ass which is hurt from being hit by a truck in March). it's still hot.

2. your tiny starfish hands are perfect for fisting. slide right in.

3. all that time spent in bed, flat on my ass, I just jerk off and jerk off and jerk off. This has been documented. It keeps my free. all that time spent in bed, another virus, pain day, fatigue day, reset sleep schedule, stiff hips in the morning, I jerk off and jerk off and jerk off. My magic wand is better than any prescription pain med I can steal a script for. I ride the pole happy, get myself off like none other. how many five million orgasms has this ass writhed around and given myself in this fibro blood red candy apple bed?

4. you squeal like a little kid when I take you to the gluten free restaurant because you know you'll be able to eat everything that's there.

5. you wash and fold my laundry washed in fragrance-free detergent when I'm flaring and unable to take time off from the two jobs or make it up and down the stairs.

6. washing dishes for you is foreplay so your rsi wrists can be strong enough to fuck me later.

7. I am twenty-nine and I am living with the girl who is supposed to be my everything forever. she doesn't think I'm really sick and I understand why. both raised poor and working class, where anything but disability the world calls obvious, you suck it up

and work and work through. her with the shards of metal in her eye from one construction site, asbestos in her lungs from another, her body lean with cigarettes and coffee. she tells me I could work more than two days a week if I really wanted to, tells me the organics I scrimp to buy because they are the only thing that brought me out of the tired years are luxury. one day in our lesbian two bedroom Victorian apartment with the wood floors, the one I moved into because it got me into a warm apartment with a bathtub that is above ground, my legs go out from under me and I fall into the shower. I scream. She doesn't come. When I come out and say, hey, didn't you hear me? she laughs at me. *Why do you make such a big deal out of everything? Why are you always freaking out?* Her laugh gives my hips no place to open under hers.

8. three balance-and-mobility challenged crips go to Hella Gay East Bay. "ok, I usually grab a bar stool and dance on it." we assess but can't drag one through the writhing masses. instead, you sit with your fake legs dangling off the stage and I dance nasty and grind between your thighs. dance with my lover like I've never danced with any partner. definitely any white partner. you slam me into the amp and make out with me while Ellery claps her hands and says "that's so hot."

9. I am thirty-four and when I start fucking you and the other one, I decide I don't want to date anyone who's not a crip ever again. Same as when the end of white boys happened, I sink gratefully into the pleasure of never having to explain. My sickness, unpredictable tides of fevers and sore hips, microtrembling butterfly hands and legs, need a strict sleep schedule, Siberian ginseng, yoga once a week that is medicine not lululemon luxury. Of moaning and cajoling and coercing, yes, there, fuck me, oh yes

sudden breaking into oh fuck! my hip! no, no! Being absolutely normal. I sink into knowing that you will never laugh shame me for being too tired to make it to the club, and I will never shame you for the pain that tops you every day all day.

9a. the pain tops you every day all day so you top all the time. you top at work at the dungeon and with your lovers. you don't let anyone touch you. when I ask you how the yoga for people with scoliosis class went you said, "it was difficult." when I ask why you say "it's difficult basically any time I try to be inside my body."

10. fibro hips like butterfly wings, that tremor tremor tremor. so fast nobody could see it. little earthquakes on the left wing, on the right wing. fibro hips like butterfly wings tremmoring. micro spasms you can see can't see. can you see it? do you know how to see it? as I hold on tight to the bus railing, inch and inch up the stairs. fibro hips that shake and shake that I do not curse and fear anymore.

dirty river girl

1.
There's an underground river flowing through every queer-of-colour community I've ever been a part of and kissed.
The underground river of kids who went away.

The girls and boys who got sick and tired, spent hours curled up sleeping.
An underground river swelling its banks
filling the riverbed
carrying us away

Fibro
chronic fatigue
lyme disease
epstein barr
cancer
endometriosis
MS,
multiple chemical sensitivity

We were all just too sensitive. Fatigue too thick to make sense of phone, Trader Joe's, Laundromat, let alone meeting, party, dance floor.

We
go
away

Sick

Sick?

you sick again? you still in bed, girl? it's three in the afternoon!

Shame makes our hips crumble to the floor
sticks us there

There's an underground river that whispers:
abuse survivors are the ones who get the weird diseases.
the ones who were raped and touched too young,
us whose bodies tell terrible stories, horrible lies.

Our bodies' walls cave in on the stories they hold that are too much swell our banks in a flash flood.

Leave us crumpled in sweatpants on our beds, vibrators always plugged in for pain control, herbal infusion in big mason jars, cell phone where we text our friends when we're too gone to call, on hold for the low-income queer clinic for sliding-scale acupuncture, again.

Sweating. Scared.

Sometimes, you never see us again.

When I was in my early twenties I was supposed to be like Zadie Smith or Saul Williams, famous and accomplished at 21 with a book or a CD, or a spoken-word celebrity. Instead, my early twenties went away. I spent them sleeping. 15, 17, 19 hours a day. That was my accomplishment.

When I was in my early twenties, I walked back into memory. Walked up the stairs of a one-bedroom apartment with a half-broken front door I could still lock. I wrote my parents my terrible story, stuck the envelope in the mailbox and walked away. I got tireder and tireder, like I had some Victorian wasting disease. Except that I wasn't Victorian, I was a light brown girl with old glasses, a bad haircut, a sick and tired body.

All I could do was sleep, so that's what I did. I slept and I reknit. Surrendered and fell. On my futon, in the hours of lying down it took to make it to the bathroom, I found the stories that felt like river stones in my belly. I could touch their smooth charcoal backs and know they were real. '

My terrible story, it was the bones I would need
What had happened to me, what had happened.

I chose to believe my terrible story.

And I healed. I healed true.

2.
When I was a little girl growing up in the rust-belt town of Worcester, Massachusetts, the river that ran through my hometown was the Blackstone, only it was more of a myth than a river. It was a river no one had ever seen. The people who had come to Worcester to work in the shoe and textile factories, leather and electronics, they knew the Blackstone because it turned the wheels of the mills that made the money for the bosses.

But in the seventies the city fathers put the Blackstone in a culvert, and it became a myth. A myth of a pretty woman who had become a monster. The Blackstone had been put to work like our working-class women's bodies, worked and worked to make someone else money, til she was worked to rags, thin and worn through, discarded when her body was too dirty for anyone to want to touch.

Entombed in cement, she slowly filled up with poison from all those dyes, all that cement, all those computer chips rinsed with acid. She flowed under the city, and we never saw her sweet hips or her cum rushing green and willowy through our beautiful rust-belt-empty lot paradise. All we knew was she was fucked up and hidden, locked up someplace where no one would touch her.

In 1983, my mother could recite the thirty-three cancer-causing compounds in Worcester water. The city fathers insisted that the water was fresh and clean, but all we knew is you could smell the chlorine thicker than a pool before you turned on the tap. Drinking it, you could feel your cells shrivel, and you knew you were forever fucked, a dirty river girl drinking dirty Worcester water that would make you too sick to even make it out. Working class folks and lower middle class ones like my mama bought bottled water, 29 cents a gallon, and we drank and drank.

It worked and it didn't. There's only so much bottled water can do. When the wind was blowing from Norton's plant, you wanted to puke at my school, 500 yards away. Every year, a teacher's hair fell out with alopecia, and another teacher got breast or colon cancer. I was 19 when my mother was diagnosed with stage 4 ovarian cancer, tentacles touching her uterus and intestines, blooming like algae in a polluted lake. The first girl I kissed grew up in Leominster, where there was a little uranium leak in the 80s. She found out she had cervical and uterine cancer at 28, when she went for her first pap smear in ten uninsured years.

And through it all, the fingers of mothers and fathers
 touching and whiskey and silence and rage, passed down.
All our bodies sick and fucked for no good reason.
Just some dumb stories we made up that no one wanted to hear.

3.
What would it take for a river that polluted
to be loved?
What would it take for us to know our bodies beautiful?
To wash them clean?

Nah—not washed clean.

What if our working-class, fucked up, sick, survivor bodies
 beautiful   just like they were?
 beautiful like the weed trees that would take over every abandoned
lot in my hometown?

What would it take for that river to be loved?

For cement to bomb open?

For my body
for your body
to come back from being swept away?

When I flare I go in my bed and I fuck myself so hard. I close all the doors and I make myself come, over and over again. Sometimes I jerk off, read library books and look at Facebook at the same time. my cock in my pussy and my vibrator on my clit stays there forever. sometime I just hover there in that place with no coming for hours, and there is no pain, just me being the slut that kept me alive.

When I fuck myself I close my eyes and think of my best friend with lyme getting caned by her daddy when she's taken enough oxy for her pain. I think of all of us fucking ourselves in our beds where we sick. when we're not. I think of how lucky I am to still get to come.

When I fuck myself, I remember: they didn't wash us away.
filthy
abandoned when not making them money anymore.
gorgeous. shaky hipped. coming.
they can't put this shit in no culvert.
we didn't go anywhere. even if you didn't visit.
she unquenchable. she here after all the bullshit done.
she keeps coming. I surrender to it. we right here.

all it takes to love a river that polluted
a body that full of story
is to surrender
to love it

I
give
in

crip sex moments

1. Cancel

When I think of my crip dating life, half of what I think of is all the times I've had to cancel.

All the times I've made plans and then realized ten minutes before I'm supposed to be there, or three hours, that I'm just not gonna make it.

All the text messages I sent when I was too tired to talk.

All the guilt-ridden messages left on someone's voicemail when I didn't know I didn't have to apologize for my body.

Dating you was crip crazy dating to the core. Our desire was punctuated by the rhythms of us canceling and rescheduling. Texts were our favourite slutty adaptive device. "Sup boo—I'm so sorry, but I'm having a fatigue crash, can we reschedule?" "Hey, sexy, I'm having a really bad panic and anxiety day, can we move our date til next week?" We cancelled and rescheduled more times then we actually managed to go out with each other.

When we made it to each other, I had some of the best dates ever with you. We were ultrabrown together sharing a lamb shawarma at the halal spot in downtown Oakland—I got my lipstick all over the pita. We broke one of the inside handles of my car making out in the front seat because your room in your 8-person queer-people-of-colour collective house didn't have a door that shut. I knew you must really like me because when I was completely grumpy about having to go to the anarchist bookfair for work on my Sunday off (and be surrounded by smelly white people with bad politics and dreadlocks), you said, "I can totally go with you, ma."

But both of our bodies were unpredictable. You kept going upstairs during parties because of your anxiety. I kept working so hard that when I came home and got into bed, capitalism had bled all the heat out of me.

We dated through our dates and through our cancellations

In the end, we trailed off into unreturned phone calls.

But I knew you would never shame my unpredictable pretty body. You're still the only desi I've made out with wearing my Tamil Women Against Genocide t-shirt. We danced so good together, brown on brown grinding for hours , and your head fit perfect into my tits.

2. Melanin night sky full of stars

When you were born, you body was covered with small brown spots. Your body is the night sky shot through with stars. The cosmos swirls all around you, your body is a roadmap to the stars. The doctors call it neurofibromitosis II. Said they'd never seen any child with so many birthmarks. You call it melanin rising. The darkness in your body, the Palestinian and African blood refusing to shut up.

When I met you, when I saw you across the cafeteria at the writers of colour retreat and knew you would be in my life for a long, long time, I didn't know you were disabled. I barely knew I was. We both knew, knew it every day waking and sleeping, behind our eyelids every day of our life, but it's not like we told anybody, or they knew how to listen. You told me haltingly about your body the second or third time we fucked. Were you worried I would reject you? Did you know that there were children with NF I called monster?

Your body a map to the stars, your spots tamarind and charcoal, on an already caramel skinned map. Gorgeous. The most gorgeous body I've ever known. I kissed every one, wound my tongue down to the creases in your ass, to the spots behind your knees, the curves released from your binder. Some days when we walked down Telegraph you folded over trying to hide from everyone who stared at you, but on the lemon yellow silk coverlet of your bed, your body flew open. You trusted me with every part of you.

Some time later, when we were having our first very tense post-breakup conversation at Albany Bulb after not speaking for a year, your phone rang. It was your doctor at the queer and trans free clinic. You said, my doctor only calls when it's bad news. I said, I'm sure it's fine. I concentrated on steering my '91 Camry through the north Berkeley streets I barely knew, until I heard you say, "I've got a tumor? On my optic nerve? Will you have to cut my head open?"

I cup your swirling beauty years after we are no longer lovers, to where we still love each other beyond imagining. My queer family, brother from another mother, we are married, or something so much better than marriage. On each others' powers of attorney for medical and financial care, sharing the same twenty-year-old car that takes our sore bones to the supermarket and sliding scale acupuncture. We pool our pain meds and hold each other in bed watching Glee on days when everything hurts, celebrate birth days and feast days. I love you in sickness and in health, til death do us part. Through your free healthy San Francisco 7 am MRIs and my biopsy results, through the days where we are both so tired.

Your cosmos is still the most beautiful one I have ever swum in.
Your heart my heart's jewel.
A supernova is a star that glows so bright, when it explodes
it briefly outshines an entire galaxy.

3. Couch flirting

I started flirting with you on Facebook from where we were both laid out on our couches. We were swallowing Vicodin, watching free internet TV and cemented to our favourite social networking site, because it's not like we could go to a party right then. I noticed you when you did that 36 Things For Invisible Illness Week meme. You wrote that your cane was the sexiest adaptive device ever, it made my nipples tighten. I posted on your wall, "My cane is brown and curvy and strong like me. Maybe our canes could go on a date?" You posted back, "I'd like that very much." And it was on.

You asked me what my favourite gluten-free treats were and brought me brownies from Mariposa Bakery. We sat on my couch and you played with my hair for hours as we talked about somatics, the burnout movement organizing jobs we'd both fled and all the obsessive faggot homemaking you were doing since you admitted you were sick after years and years and left your youth organizer 80-hour-a-week job. My pussy was so wet you could've driven a cruise ship through it.

My breasts ached for you but there was something so hot about our trauma-and-abuse flirtation, about how we were moving so, so, slow.

Your house was so cripped out you had a couch in every room! You said, "Of course I have four couches! Honey, my chronically ill ass needs to lie down as much as possible!" My house was so cripped out there was a space heater in every room and I blasted them constantly, even though it pissed my roommate off and made her pro-rate the energy bill. I wanted you so bad I made my whole wardrobe and body product line fragrance-free in the hopes that when we made out I wouldn't give you a seizure.

I wanted to fuck you on every couch in your house.

I wanted to take you to my big crip bed and just not get out for days and days. Just dissolve into the deliciousness of lying down with someone else who knew what it was like to always lie down.

You ended up being too deep into somatics and trauma to do it, but there was still something so sweet home about the giant wheat-free brunches you made for me, cuddling on all the couches, all your texts when I was the only crip on tour and my body felt like it was dying that comforted me to the bone.

Dating you made me never want to date anyone but another crip ever again.

this is what I know about crazy

Crazy fam, before anything else, I want to say, I love you. I love us. I am loyal to us with the first sunrise and the last sunset. I will stand and sit for us. Give me the worst, the most secret shit crusted moment, and it will not be too much for me. I will touch it gently, with my best honour. Wrong is not our name, was never our name, not in our worst moments hiding in the toilet trying to convince ourselves not to flush ourselves down it.

the thing I wanted to say about crazy is:

1. there is nothing wrong with you
2. it still sucks sometimes
3. you gotta figure out a way to love yourself anyway
4. it's a daily practice. we're all really good at that
5. most folks won't want you to talk about it why?
5.5 cause it freaks them out or their shit out or reminds them of them or they can't understand how you're saying it out loud. wtf is wrong with you are you crazy?
6. cause if you grew up in a family like mine or even if you didn't. talking about it meant you might be taken away somewhere. . . forever
7. crazy lockups have to do with ableism and the prison industrial complex and poverty. if we're a freak we're stared at and lockedaway. we're some of the threat, all of the time
8. you can still grow between the cracks. punch out space in your chest for a liberated zone. be in bed as much as you fucking want. take the pills don't take the pills.

you're going to find the people you can sketch the secret inside of the world with. if you can't find them you can sketch the secret inside of your world inside yourself. breathe in the place where all the words fall away into lemon yellow rose fractals and it's fucking amazing.

9. there's treasure there and there's also rocks

10. I don't believe it's just a symptom or biochemistry but if you do, it's ok. I will stand with my people for whatever keeps us alive

11. your crazy is beloved genius art when you're not standing on the tracks trying not to jump, and when you are. . . that's different.

12, it gets better it doesn't get better it just changes it gets better it doesn't get better it just changes

what I want to say about crazy is:

1. my people have always been crazy

but our crazy isn't that beloved crazy of fancy white dead men
our crazy is just crazy
dirty
innocent
writhing

when we love ourselves it's dirty
underground
and gorgeous

we're feared and hated and loved
by cops, doctors

and our famillies
people on the street when we don't pass
and queerfamily
who is scared
sometimes we fear and hate and love ourselves
all at the same time

2. when I lose language and words it's so innocent. wrong is never the name when I don't see the word tree, i see the tree, I see the sky. I see everything as it is. I see colour and scent and music, I see everything before words. this is my first language. nothing is wrong with it. it doesn't allow me to get on the bus. I am translating every single word I am saying to you from that first language. this is not a metaphor. you don't believe me. I'm so articulate. I got a really high score on my verbal SATs. I had to, but my first language is the palace of colours and scent and being. and I'm not lying to you, and the worst thing you could do when i'm in it, when finding every fucking word is like climbing a fucking mountain, is to laugh.

3. the ones for whom nothing is too much are precious. treasure them your best treasure.

4. sometime you will forget that not everyone knows the inside of crazyworld. you'll wake up with a start when you realize there are those whose brains never melted, who have never kissed the inside lip of the mouth of the gun of trauma. you will start awake at their stares. how can they not know this world? isn't it written on the inside lip of everything.

5. there are many people who know the inside of crazyworld, but they are hiding more than even we are. we are all hiding to a

certain degree to survive this world. i don't want to be locked up or stared at and I want to have friends and a job, so I have practiced how to smile and ask for an english breakfast tea just right. I do a really good job of it. That's why you want me to come to your college to do some gay performance art, isn't it?

6. my mom taught me all about holding it together and then having private time to fall the fuck apart. even when you're working class and that time is fiveminutes locked in your car. my mom taught me about box gallo white wine, her recliner, and yr and lifetime television for women. basically a single mom with a husband who didn't fuck her, two jobs, a mom who couldn't drive anymore who was taking a long time to die in the social security housing complex for seniors in webster mas. my mom had no pleasure. and a lot of crazy. and a lot of splits in her brain, and she held it the fuck together until it was time to go home to the house she was paying the mortgage on, all by herself. and she did it without therapy or drugs or friends.

I was the little girl who read anne landers, and used to say to her, mommy, can we go to family therapy some day? and she would hold her hand back like she was going to slap me in the face, but she wouldn't, because she was better than her mother and say: what the fuck is wrong with you what kind of people do you think we are do you want to get taken away somewhere?

7. internalized ableism is the worst and half of us don't even know that word. but it's that voice that tells you you are making it all up, you need to get the fuck out of bed, what the fuck is wrong with you, why is it so hard there's nothing wrong with you, you're a hypochondriac, this is fucking nothing, that's not what pain feels like. buck up buck up buck up.

you can't just buck up.
sometimes we rise anyway.
so often we rise anyway.
so often we go to work anyway

there is no nest. sometimes.

gotta be hard to be in this world

tree. sky. concrete. library.

what

what

what would movements made with our brains in mind look like?
what do we know? what do we have that no one else has
why were we made in this perfect image by a god who loves crazy
boys and girls and othergenders
and how do I dance with the ideation so it doesn't take me out?

these are the things I love about crazy

how we're still here
this brain shattered into a million beautiful fractal raindrops
the high of synthasia
the way you can lick the inside of your skull
the manic flight and the deep grief sacred low when you feel the
heartbreak of this world

this is how harriet tubman knew what path by the stream to walk
to freedom with by starlight

this is how my mother knew the pilot light went out and and gas
was filling the house
how she knew the drunk driver was around the corner
this is how i knew the pilot light was off inside my body and it
was filling with gas and something was terribly wrong
the way watching angel haze flash her wrist scars on youtube is
like cocaine for me
the only time I have seen someone who looked sort of like my life
on a youtube channel

dear crazy kin
we are the ones whose brains light up and go out
we're this way due to oppression and abuse
but we are also like this because our brains are fucking weird
and maybe we are the secret
and maybe we're just these crazy people trying to get through
    the day
maybe don't pay any mind to the poems others write about us
none of them are as sacred
as the poem
of us,
of the poem we write
of ourselves.
We are my favorite poem
I
love
us

where I would find you
for Laura Hershey

the slow/walking lane of the Berkeley Y
you on the wheelchair lift, me walking slow, slow
 all of us on our low-income memberships.
The elevator of every BART station,
any elevator, anywhere
any ramp, any time
 any house where we bed bound jail break time
the community acupuncture clinic waiting room
my friend's living room
where she exquisitely tops her PCA about precisely which dish
   to use
and gifts me with the ability to lift her palm—

I mean the Facebook invite I didn't notice or say yes to
til after you died. I mean
every place my hips hurt, I mean
every sweet sweet drooling cripfemme kiss,
I mean every equation of 12-72 hours rest time for
four hours storming the port of Oakland,
I mean every access van lineup
every argument on Facebook about where is the access info, again
I mean every moment we angry not grateful
every moment illuminated by your words' grace

every time my voice shakes reading the last line
of the last poem you wrote

I mean, I did not find you til after you passed

RSI

when you fucked me extra hard with your wrist braces like
corsets for hands
when you rubbed my arms with arnica
and said *oooh, baby, you're about to get what I have*
from years of landscaping and graphic design
when you were right and you brought over your extra braces
switched to pot balm
used the tips of your elbows to rub the pain out of my forearm
    cramps
bought me dragon naturally speaking for my birthday early
I was grateful
I am grateful
I am grateful
a gratitude
that wouldn't dismember me

that all my body
and all yours
got to love each other
without changing a goddamn thing

iv. hard girls

etymology of tough girl heart #2

1.
booty shorts tough ass swish swash
stomp cut like butter
violin me songs on hipbone's saw

look at me cut this sidewalk
hot knife through
hot butter
look at me make it melt
look at me make a way
look at me

2.
your ribs are like a corset
and the softness of your tits
is also part of the armour
we teach with our tits and our hard
hard breastbone
nothing gets in
we don't want to
they're a challenge
they're a dare

3.
your ribs are a corset
wrapped round and round your pericardium
and that bomb heart ticks inside
sore
lovely
your ribs are a corset

holding you up
brocade'n silk leather
lets you scratch sky, boo—

and your ribs waitwaitwait
for the moment the string gets pulled
and that leather
finally
drops

I love hard girls
for amber dawn

hips like a hummingbird jackhammer
a brick house   body a brick city
crumbling
Boots that climb to thighs
thick and pebbled
with the big bags of potatoes and rice waiting in the pantry
to survive hard times
Those girls who will fuck you up for no good reason

I love girls with whiskey espresso belly
I love the brown girl worry line
perpendicular to the perfect eyebrow
The rosewater olive oil in the food and in the homemade facial
    toner
the groupon and the gas money
the twenty bucks tucked away and passed
the penny jar hip bones shaking brass
the emergency stockings
the you wanna make $300?

The delicious satisfaction of wanting to text
go fuck yourself
I hate you
fuck you

I love girls who wanna set shit on fire,
whose cut eye can penetrate oil spills
I love girls who want to smash faces, break windows
whose asses swish with the cut of razors

I love every loud-mouthed-hard-assed-fuck-with-you
skin soft like a loquat as they punch your cunt into an infinity
    femme
I love girls who will fuck you up for no
and every good reason

and I love those girls
who look at me hard and whisper *thank god*
who have never once been scared of me

hussyflower

1.
girlfemme heartfemme heartsister sistergirl:
you not here
but you live in my ovarian cyst
you live in my cancer scare
a baby not born bomb cradle lodged in my womb's side
You an unwritten letter   a curse word won't leave my lips
a rant not worth it to spill
You an egg divided and divided
won't become a baby
You my first breath when I wake, my last lights out.

2.
when she breaks your heart

hussy flower femmes know best how to break heart
she will write you an elegantly restrained bitch letter
she will set your house on fire with words
you will remember her a year later
when she has left her job, left town, gone to Oaxaca
lives in a photo on your desk of you two grinning huge shark
    grins
you will remember her a year later
in another thick meat jawed femmepomp sideburns
rosette earrings side shave
in front of you at the show
you will remember her
how could you ever forget her?
femmes like you are unforgettable
that's the whole point

mash note

Our song was *she makes me feel like the only girl in the world*
only I think I was the only one of us
who knew it was our song

when she fucked me on pride day hot toronto bed
I cried because my cunt felt rusty
she texted me later
such an honour to fuck such a powerful woman on pride day
and then
I'm on MDMA
but it still counts

said finally
I like dating white men because I can kind of check out
with you I have to be present and that's real hard

the first girl I bought a dozen lavender roses for her birthday
and mailed them to her in the snow

getting high from unlimited texts like cocaine and dopamine

and when it's over it's over
the quickest five sentence skype breakup ever
years later you will twerk your ass in her face by accident
she feed you til you not hungry til you hungry til you gone

enough

In June, I run away from the Bay. The past six months have felt like getting kicked in the chest, by a horse, over and over again. I work three jobs and seven days a week. I work 12 hour days bookended by hour-long commutes. At the end of them, I emerge from the BART station, walk to where my aging station wagon sits in disabled parking, drive the five blocks home, limp up the stairs, microwave something from Trader Joe's for dinner, watch Glee, jerk off and pass out. I don't even come hard, I just masturbate half-heartedly until I come enough to be able to sleep.

I am worn out to the bone and everything is a panic attack crisis. Whenever I'm not working, I am recovering—going to yoga or community-based acupuncture, trying to catch up with all the friends I owe phone calls to, lying in bed on painkillers in a Soma/tv on the internet haze when I have a flare, which is often, canceling plans so I can sleep. I am supposed to have a flexible lifestyle and work habits that allow my chronically ill body to thrive. Instead, I have this.

I go to sleep thinking that I am just like my mom— an overworked, bone-tired, disabled working-class woman who is busting her ass for a small paycheck and a collapsed body. The ovarian cyst that always comes up when I am grieving and underfucked comes back; so does mid-cycle bleeding. I used to not worry so much in my twenties, but I am 35 now and I worry I will have cancer like my momma soon. Although I keep repeating how blessed I am—and I am, I have friends and love, and when the really bad crises come, like my car getting booted and me needing $1,000 in 48 hours, I get the loans—there's a lot that is just bad. I have weeks where I wake up praying that this will be a calm week, and by the end of Monday, I know it is not. In the middle of all this, I lose my two best femme friends of colour, a lover is hit by a drunk driver while on her bike and is severely disabled for six months, and a project that's been at the centre of my life's work is dissolving. There is a cancer scare, dates who can't do more than kiss, verbally abusive coworkers, the Oscar Grant trial, the Gulf oil spill, e-mails waiting for me telling me what a fuckup I am. Free Will Astrology explains that Uranus is conjunct whatever and it's a time of transformation, but still, fuck this. Fuck this sobbing from the gut, exhaustion, empty, lonely, loss.

I don't want it. I want to be a grown-up femme with a lovely laugh, running her life, wind between her thighs.

Some nights I go to bed crying because my belly is round, my pussy is wet, there is all this goodness just going to waste. I could live without sex, I have lived without so much. It's not like I'm going to die without it. People live without fucking all the time. It's not like I'm going to die without it. I've lived without so much. Except that something is dying. Except that I feel like I'm dying. Without it, without joy, without enough.

When I see her, I think: I can just reach out and kiss you and it'll be okay. She jumps to carry my big fuchsia suitcase when I walk into our mutual best friend's performance night. I kiss her goodbye, get hot pink lipstick all over her face, and rub it off her lips hard, almost a slap. She looks so happy.

When we finally have our date, it is slow and enough. I sit on her lap, thick brown thighs spread around her, laced up in dark cherry corset boots, lime green panties with little brown polka dots spread wide. It's not vanilla sex—she slaps my breasts and watches my face as I throw my head back, sway and pulse my hips into her cock—but I could kiss her for hours, and I do. She puts her face in my breasts so slow, exhales when she pulls down the cups and sees my nipples for the first time. She asks if she's taking too long playing with my nipples with her lips and tongue, when I say hell no says thank god, my last girlfriend hated it when I took forever, I could kiss your breasts for hours. When she fucks me—she has "Daddy's Girl" tattooed on her calf, and the S is a dollar sign, and she is, but I top her into daddying me and she gives me what I want. She fucks my pussy that's so tight after six months of nothing, says, you are so tight little girl, open up for me, that's right—and I don't have to work to come. And I cry when I do cause it's like all the pain, all the not-enough, all the worked-to-death worn-through tired crip body, is coming out of my pussy onto her hands when she gives me what I have needed for so long.

Later, she texts me, "I could tell you needed to be fucked so bad and I was so happy to be able to give that to you."

And then there was the moment on Skype where she said, "Only the hottest girls have fibromyalgia" and I threw back my head and laughed and laughed and fell in love.

because every brown femme needs/
where you find homegirl medicine

1.
sometimes medicine nothing more or less than that one ciara cut on repeat after you both say *I think we need to break up* on skype, you all ice fire in veins, snapping fingers slamming out bacon buttermilk biscuits and a maple buttermilk pie. nothing but a dry fire of rage ache, needle on the gauge of gone.

sometimes when you make your gratitude list it's all the missy and azalea remix of m.i.a.'s bad girls, your sistergirl's $900 2-bedroom above one of five dollar stores bloor-and-ossington (*I will be hanging on to this apartment til I am dead.*) her rust broken tail bone bottle banging laughter, her little tiny joint smoked cutting across duffy grove on the way to a stoned ardene mission, how you get asked sisters, how you cut eye and say yes. both your matching curls going white right in the front. she has a law degree and unemployment, you have a cv, a lavender roller wheel suitcase from overstock.com, dual citizenship and a precariously stable career as an itinerant queer brown cis disabled poet, hips sore on every plane. the gratitude that is rust brown laughter and a million hair flowers and a million broken beautiful bitches in a clothing swap, stripper heels and space heaters on high and yes girl, get that, you need that, yes. it's the taco truck and the tea garden, it's homegirl laughter on a couch is where you can always come home.

2
sometimes you get real quiet. you don't know how to write an elegy for yourself. you 38 and still crazy. you want to rocket back to 2009, 2010, 2011 or 12. before fukushima blew up spit poison

in the ocean always your salve mother five minutes away, before your best friend stopped talking to you, before you fell in love and were changed, back when you still felt young inside. you know your words are like every indie rapper's third album. it's weird at the not really top.

You and her, you met in 1997 in a sanjaytown basement. before cell phones, legal immigration status. before 9/11 you were still not meant to survive. you had just had a huge fight with a lover on the subway where you got real young and couldn't talk. fifteen years later you are beyond the shock of arrival, you know what to do when that happens, you find your way back to the palace of words. you walked in to that basement filled with DMO Theatre, that radical Lankan theatre collective of dishwashers who used to be teachers and engineers like your grandparents, saw her. You said, "Are you Burgher?" loud and rude. She said, "No." She is Indian by way of Guyana with a white mom. You said, "Do you even know what that means?" She said, "Yes." You looked at her and nodded. The point is you recognized each other. Before you had words.

3.
A year and change after your former best friend breaks up with you via the internet, it makes you closer to leaving your body permanently than you ever have wanted. You fight the urge to leave to try and make things right, you fight the urge whispers, *you must be really fucked up* to hurt him and for him to offer no reparation plan, no way back, no transformative justice, didn't you write the book on that. only thing you can think to do is you should take yourself off the planet.

Thinking of the people who love you, who you love, doesn't work so great. his name meant the best, you whispered best friend family forever, his name on your power of attorney and will, what will it be like if you kill yourself and he gets to dispose of your assets. If your words took him away, maybe breathing and sending meta every morning like your great-great-grandmother maybe did, won't bring him back, but it is breathing and sending meta every morning.

4.
what medicine do we looklong for?

hopper hut hoppers in another kennedy ellesmere strip mall.
kottu rotty at the storefront all night.
here, we search for unrotted mangos and greens.
a seawater bed. lapping and chatting.
medicine watching kat williams and giving up and hitting the one hitter twice.
medicine the purple couch in the purple house. some shitty sweet red wine.
traced alphabet we ashamed we only know half of.
grit and dirt. gristle. meat and greens. the courage to cut.
the knowledge grasped of what is cut and what is carving.
three drops of a remedy called I Am Ready For Love
clutch your quartz-like pearls like rosary, girl. heart open.

5.
we heal with tinctures made out of sweat, jupiter, butterscotch
    and eclipse.
we heal with salt packets and microwaved motel water
we heal with youtube mixes named too blessed
we heal bleeding and pissing in the dirt outside my house

we got rocks from the city park and purses full of tincture
we got unlimited text messaging crisis line up all night
we got the two ancestor pictures made it off the boat
we got skin   we got the dancefloor
got little dresses/ big boots

got white hair and a neat line of floggers
got breath.

we got how i know how to call your name
and how we know the name of the land we live on

6.
homegirl medicine: the duffy mall hm, the grass of the baby bowl, the long alleyway railroad tracks to rose's house. the secret map of the inside of the brown world. you always find home here. home on the thin arched bone of ciara, your girls, the railroad tracks where you've always rented an apartment.

are you still a hard femme, love? or are you so soft, broken open by the world?

I will take care of you forever

spring equinox and I wake at six a.m. because you're not standing
on my chest
but something is hovering. I turn the light on. edit what I wrote.
I feel you pass out of right ovary
I don't have to hold on to you.
there's no way I could lose you
I whisper, *I don't think I ever told you*
the Cree word for love means we'll take care of each other forever
and even though we'll never speak again
I promise: this to you.

v. wrong is not yours

insh'allah
for harsha walia

We hug hard for five minutes on a Vancouver couch.
You lift me up. Giddy gloss of joy.
Were you in Detroit, boo?
Nah, girl, I can't cross the border! No border for me!
you chirp. Scream so loud when I tell you our friend played with
my nipples for three hours.
I flash you my bra so you'll talk before me at our gig so I can
soak up your light
before you go running to another plane to another BDS confer-
ence.
*My wedding is in four days! Maybe if it was a demonstration
it'd be planned! I can't even walk down the block without the
  cops yelling at me!*
This border is rotten meat, a hallucination, a wavering line
a stupid idea. Can't we blink and it'll be gone?

Stick your toe over it, back.
Stick your tongue out at the border.
You wave your fingers in a heart around your chest
point it at me,
we hug each other tight on this couch, on this unceded territory
of each other
on the island of forty-seven minutes we have.
I say *I'll see you soon you say I hope you will sweetie, I hope*
I say, *I'm holding you in my heart*
travel safe to the BDS conference, girl
insh'allah
brown girl wings wrap around you, sister
brown girls wings hold us safe

lift us flying laughing uproarious brown girl birds flapping wings over the border
thumbing noses and laugh cracking crow throats
insh'allah

wrong is not yours
after June Jordan

for all of us with beautiful long names from the homelands, especially those of us who got them in adulthood

one day you are a 22-year-old with dreadlocked half-desi hair you decided to lock when you did double dip mescaline on new year's eve after staring at pictures of sadhus in south india. years before Carol's Daughter or Palmer coconut hair milk or Kinky Curly in Target and you have no idea what to do with all that curly curly hair

who decides you wants to change her name from albrecht no more albrecht   you want your great-grandmothers   you are a 22-year-old on a straight diet of franz fanon marlon riggs and chrystos   you are a sri lankan christian daughter of the dutch east india company you want no more albrecht no more rape in your pelvis no more *where'd you get that name* no more *are you adopted* no more

even through yr grandmas whisper   *keep a white name for the passport   keep as many passports as possible   you never know what boat you're going to have to get on   who you'll have to bullshit in an immigration office
you never know where we'll have to run to   make home in sip your tea   cook your rice   wait for death looking at an ocean that almost looks like yours*

but you want your great-grandmother's name who means hot pepper   who walked out of the galicia with 13 children your other great-grandmother whose name is a footnote in a

lankan history book's cross-referenced index you find researching
yr senior thesis on mixed-race women in sri lanka   teachers
union organizers and sluts everyone of us
and you get something infinitely googleable and infinitely
unpronounceable except for ukrainians and lankans and dravidians

and even when dennis kucinich runs for president
and puts an mp3 file on his website saying how to say his name
and you think it might be a good idea too
your name is not wrong
wrong is not your name
it is your own
your own
                              your own
your own
your own

airport ode #1

The truth is, I ask for the opt out.
I ask for it every time.
I would rather be patted down by a 60ish white working class
woman who looks like my mom
who I will studiously ma'am and ask about her day,
than to sit sweating waiting for it to happen.
Than to have that beam of atoms shot through my body
and still get barked aside, patted down,
tarot cards, cock and coconut oil wanded.

Once on my way to a redeye from a performance in a cocktail
dress you were young and brown and queer
and you said damn, *it'll be easy to search you,*
you're hardly wearing anything at all
You complemented my mukkuthi
and because I am a frequent queerartbrownlady flyer
you remembered me from a week or two ago

This is where we are in 2012:
I chat friendly and deliberate with the sister
who searches me
legs spread one in front of the other, back of the hand on sensitive
areas
your zipper line, your bra
casual spread-eagle in public
as everyone hops on shoes, puts laptops back

Not too long ago, every airport line a panic attack, every airport
four hours sweating armpit rank,
every bus crossing the small room and barking guards who don't

ever pretend to be polite
who go through all your things and take you to the glass toilet
Every time they chirp or bark, "I'm going to pat your hair"
I go deep inside and all the way out.

Once, my girlfriend picked me up at the airport with a little tupperware of dinner
and fucked me in long-term parking bent over the hood of your car
I was too nervous to come but I loved
how she wanted to feed me,
how she wanted to fuck me back
in the middle of all these
concrete cameras wands scanners fingerprints nexxus
red blinking eye

this place
that hates us

what it's like to be sri lankan in 2012
for those of you who aren't

It's being dead.
It's still being alive.

It's No Frills finally has Dilmah.
It's buying four packages to take home in your carry-on
because you live in the Bay Area now.
It's the Scar.
It's Little Jaffna.

It's silence
It's enormous fights on the internet on every page that purports
to be about Sri Lanka from a multicultural perspective

It's being on a raft that takes you from Jaffna to Malaysia to
Christmas Island,
to immigration jail in Australia, then somehow you bust out,
and you get to Fruitvale, Oakland, California,
on a raft,
because someone Googlemapped it
and it looked pretty.

It's small boats in big water.
It's fake buddhist temples constructed in Jaffna by the government
It's going home and seeing bullet holes in your grandmother's
empty house
It's lighting 23 candles in her window
one for every one who's died since you and everyone
have not been able to return.
It's *the government won't let us say the word trauma in the camps*

It's going home to Jaffna if you're young, Tamil and male and not automatically being snatched by either army.

It's creepy child molesting uncle,
drunkass uncle at the wedding singing baila with sexually inappropriate lyrics
it's all your aunties wanting to change the subject

It's an empty, broken heart hoping that the tears/ the rivers/
the ocean/ all that wet
will fertilize the seeds
hidden/deep/ in darkness
still to be born

It's wanting to talk about something else
It's still being alive.

how it happens

because in new york
people just look both ways when it's a red light
and if nothing's coming, they cross the street anyway

because I look up and I can see how easily everything could crumble,
how this street could look so different in an instant

because you push and push and meet and organize and
    conference call
and publish and travel and take busses and stay up late and go to bed early
and the front of you hair goes white and the 90s were twenty years ago

and one day, three thousand of your friends sit in a bowl of light
in front of the big limestone building government
and decide to all stop working and going to school next week

and you are living in the Starhawk dream of your teenagerhood
but so much less fucked up: your backyard full of chickens and greens,
house falling down pretty, bursting with busy housemates,

sweeping your hand up the falling-down stairs you will fix yourself

maestra teacher:
a rebel teacher manifesta song in many parts.

start here. or here. or here:

because you buy your youth who's locked up poetry books using your 30% discount from the anarchist bookstore you used to work at when you were hood rich after a successful run of tarot card reading even though two weeks ago you had $37 in the bank.

because you are the kind of community scholar who will always live in a movement house and rarely in an ivory tower.

because you knew you would grow up to live in a movement house.

because the movement buys you plane tickets and pays your rent.

because when you are in an ivory tower or a community college you are an insistance that we belong wherever we want to be.

because when the queer students union and the rape crisis center and the women's centre and the multicultural alliance and ethnic studies and (mayyyyybe) the english department and the disabled students union all throw in $150 each to bring you bumrush the ivory tower and jailbreak students for you to give free lectures which will be the ones the students remember all year and next year and that makes them want to start something marvelous instead of getting a Master's.

because you are the kind of teacher who drives her 22-year-old car across the bridge to teach her kids instead of flying to new york for the fancy award ceremony, and finds out she wins the fancy gay grammies literary award while on said bridge and screams and almost rearends a prius.

because one of your sweeties does a book drive for your youth who is in the prison and hops in her friend's car's passenger seat to drive down from portland to give you the books and kiss you.

because there is always room for someone else in your car.

because you are a community rolodex aunty lifesaver who also turns her phone off so she can take a salt bath, jerk off, watch netflix and dream big and deep.

because of how you say boo boo. sugar. sweetie. sweet pea. honey pie. kid. hey star. hey glitter genius. how you doing? no, how you really doin? did you guys break up? no, mama, ask for $500, not $50! you got this! have you eaten? can I get you some water? do you need a ride? do you need to talk? do you want one of five million herbal tinctures in my purse?

because you teach with your tits and your tie. your gender is one of your best gifts to your students. you show them another way to be girl or boy that is hope lodged right by their gallbladder.

because of how you chant

you got this you got this you got this
i got you i got you i got you i got you

because teaching your youth how to steal copies from Office Max and office supplies from crap data entry jobs is part of your curricula.

because you publish books. teach in living rooms, jails and lecture halls. leave zines on the bus.

because your youth not killing themselves and growing up to be happy queers who make art is your PhD and your MacArthur Genius

Because you will still get a real MacArthur Genius. Just like Octavia did.

the toronto ode suite

1. Dear Toronto: this, a love letter to you.

Dear Toronto:
I miss you.
I miss you like our parents missed home when they came here.
I miss you, because you are my home like that.

Here, everything is right. The way it should be:
Flocks of brown girl birds swarming and settling on an H&M $5 rack
The regular halal chicken $2 a pound
Here, everything is right, and I make sense of the world:
Dollarama. Library. Tucked away alley.
Ripe plums falling. Beef patties.

In California where I moved to get ahead, get an ocean and sky
I will always find myself muttering:
The produce is too ripe, sun too bright, sky an insistent annoying
    blue
I miss the smog
and dusty non-glamourous Mennonite chicken and apples
at the same corner store where the same old lady has called me
bella for fourteen years

I became grumpy aunty here
Wishing for yr smoggy cigarette-dripped-dirty-ashed perfect imperfection
Best roti in town, second city low self-esteem
and haterade for days.
Every shitty basement apartment

every fucked-up 50ish Portuguese man with sun damage and a DuMaurier clamped between his lips, riding a junker 3-speed the wrong way up St Clarens.
every Dionne Brand book tucked into Eglinton library's shelves

The good beer and bad cigarettes
the overpriced whiskey and brief lush season of nightshades and greens
I could get lost here
but instead
I find
myself

2. *TSA: we search bags randomly for the protection of the nation. today, yours was chosen*

calling card tucked between duty-free and cocks like a love note

right of customs card eyeball
to $48 flatrate cab with an uncle
who will ask me *your flight was good, miss?* until it is clear I am passing out
to the other house with a wheelchair ramp on my old block
with no lock   with a bed waiting for me
in a silver david bowie bedroom, with cats who know my name.

sleep in the first bed in a house that smells like humans in a week,
sleep til 2. hop the transit to right to dance. *step kick step.*
make your twirl tight. walk tall. walk like you're walking towards something you want.
I know everyone there. we smile. I've avoided the past five years' drama. my youth queer married
grown up, small dogs, qtpoc dance companies.
home. tattooed on my chest's breathplate and here.
parka parka, impeccable brow threading. parka. parka.
kicks toothbrushed pure every evening of salt.

ossington subway, delaware exit, scamming the weekly pass. running into family every fifth heartbeat. working hard doing real things. the rent. thrumming beat of capital.
the ever steady beat of gentrification is real
but the hood is still covered in five layers of gum, dumaurier ashes and shit. makes up for $4 coffee, bright new gallery. my footsteps beat a path here.

and when I return, everyone says *it's like you never left*
and when I return, everyone says, *you're here!*

3. *the immigrant suburbs*
for leroi newbold

we can't drive the CRV on the highway because DWB.
an hour of telling siri to shut up later, we're here:
kennedy and ellesmere, the Hopper Hut

I cover my tattoos and we bring the baby.
crab curry for $6.50 and as many milk hoppers as we can fit,
we have a black and brown queer art business meeting
the two men at the next table, who could be either of our uncles
smile at the baby and stare forward at the wall

across the parkinglot, there is a giant clean supermarket like god
 I scream when I see they have Dilmah 100s. All the Suraj
ninety nine cent homeland spice and giant Mr Goudas' and Cedar
bags of everything. $8 GF baking mix tucked next to the diaper
bag. Don't tell.
The Ukrainian checkout lady smiles at us for once.

outside, *shit are we fenced in? yeah*
but there's a hole at the edge of the parking lot

where we cane buggy stroller eight bags haul
next to two twins and their beige dove scarf momma walk through
holding hands hesitant
 a dakarite father and his son
stroll towards the endless rings of endless towers:

there is grey here, there is order, there is lockdown
abundance, there is home here.

vi. what kind of ancestor do you want to be?

My Father, Christmas 1991, As I Come Down the Stairs in Ripped Jeans and That Jane's Addiction T-Shirt With All the Naked People on It

a persona poem, for my beautiful, complicated, queer Sri Lankan dad. Thank you for making me who I am.

I am tense
I want her to take off those ripped jeans, that obscene t shirt
and put on something else.
It's Christmas
and this is not what I wanted for my life
- this little wrenlike woman I am married to,
this angular glaring daughter one shade lighter than me,
who hates me in her terrible green hair.

I want a drink.
I want to be alone in the basement,
with my heavy tumbler of Johnnie Walker Red, the history channel on low
something educational about Winston Churchill
some nice white man from the country that was the last place
I felt alive and happy
which was twenty years ago
The dull humid cool of the beige factory outlet wall-to-wall,
the old brown and orange nylon plaid couch,
my Heavy Metal comic books
and a bar painted thick brown
that nobody uses but me

I don't want to be near my parents either.
I don't want to think about them, or write them back
to their thin blue aerogram letters from Australia

or pick up the phone when they call
in the tiny window between our time zones and half a world away
where we are both awake

I don't want to think about my desire,
or how I tell the neighbors I am Portuguese,
or how far away I am from everything I knew
I lock it all in a box, my gender, my history, my parents,
all the islands I grew up on,
to live in this vinyl siding house surrounded by people I hate,
snow I hate
everything I hate but beer, TV, and silence

It's easy enough to put one foot in front of another
through my days
of paycheck, and then no paycheck,
and fuming twisting barking orders
at this wife who works two jobs when I can't find any
and puts a line of pillows down the middle of the bed
so we never touch
but I sleep in the basement, so I can masturbate in peace
and wake up to take the commuter train to someplace
that is at least a city, at least civilized
with coffee, and men I can look at
in the bathroom of Filene's Basement on my lunch break

but there she comes, this angry brown daughter
who looks sort of like me, except she despises me
for how I drive the car too fast, shout her down for all her smart-
ass remarks.
I don't know if she knows I learned to drive
the week before her mother gave birth to her

there were always trishaws, busses and the London Underground
where I grew up.
I try to talk to her in the car as she turns up the volume of her
yellow Walkman
so loud she can't even hear my voice

I know one day soon, as soon as she is done getting through
college,
the way I couldn't, she is going to go to another country
with a big bag of clothes and a notebook, just like I did,
and not take our calls, answer our letters
She will go one step further and change her phone number, unlist
it from the book,
change her name to some thing she says is both of ours
she found researching her senior thesis,
which I could've told her
if she just asked.

I think she will like women,
or like tender leaning boys who I would've liked to like too
 like the one with his ringlets who shows up at the house
with a hash brownie and roses for her.
My daughter is going to leave me here, with this silence,
johnnie walker red, the history channel on low
the wren-like woman getting quieter and quieter
my daughter is going to write a letter saying things
I never dared to say to my parents
and close the door of the basement
gently,
firmly
in my face

when people ask me the last time i saw my mother

I don't tell them about the last time because I don't
remember it. I tell them about the next to last time

say, the last real time I saw my mom was christmas 1996
when she cut off most of my hair and shoved it in a snowbank

It took me seventeen years
to hear she was starting to die

for me to lie in my bed and realize
that if my daughter ever got head lice and I had to cut her hair off

I would take her to the salon of her choice
say, *oh, sweetie, I know this sucks*

pet her head   do anything
to help her know she was still beautiful
I would comfort her

all the things we survive here,
all the work

business casual skirt, kicks, white streaked pomp and nice lady eyes:
I look nothing like my mother

all the love poured into me to walk away from that moment
where I stopped

and where I started

what kind of ancestor do you want to be?
with thanks to Indira Allegra

my mom was rude to sales clerks
was too afraid to chat easy
power locked all the doors
was afraid she'd get jumped

I grew up
to be that lady who tips 30%
sits on her stoop with her coffee
in booty shorts and a leopard print coat and wild-assed bed hair
and no bra
saying hi and yelling at all the kids on the block

I grew up to be the lady
who says please and thank you
yes ma'am and yes sir
cracks a joke
and says, *you look really nice today*
here's a dollar
how you doing?

who throws clothing swaps and dinners
and has a bunch of chickens in the freezer at all times
extra rice and beans and pain meds and a heating pad
and blankets and couches
for anyone who needs them

my mama would clutch her purse at me
think I'm low class

but being nice to receptionists, flight attendants, janitors and
waitresses
gives you all kinds of magic
noticing folks means they notice you back
give you something on the house
hook you up
and
it just makes you feel good

my mama will probably die
cause she doesn't have the hook-up

because every kind of white fear told my mama
if you're nice to brown folks
they'll kill you
they'll take the little you have
you should just become middle class
even though you hate those fuckers
even though
they will always hate you

it told her if she relaxed her grip on her purse
she'd be a dead body
not that she could get a smile if she gave one
commiseration
a free drink
not
that it would feel good

but me I'm her daughter
and I grew up to be that aunty
grey and pink hair and a tight red skirt

all loud-assed
tipping good and telling you you look really nice today
sipping my coffee in green terry booty shorts and a leopard print coat
on my stoop

and me
I do it
for both of us

sternum
for Yashna Padamsee

in the backyard at the u.s. social forum
sweaty detroit night
we were all exhausted from 10 days
of 20,000 people in the streets and no AC
desi circle in the corner of the field
behind the old navy men's bar queerdanceparty
yashna said she was coming back from new delhi
driving all her shit to oakland from durham
I asked her where home was
she stopped perfect silent in the middle of writhing screaming
queers
smiled
said *home? home is right here*
and touched her chest light

a year later
when you drilled the needle into my chest
and tattooed home there
I got high right away
you were hitting bone and heart chakra
the tattoo gun gave off smoke
I knew getting this piece would make everyone
stare at my tits even more than they did already
you said *do you want to use white ink so it doesn't show as much?*
then wait, what color is home?
we mixed ink the color
of red brown sri lankan road dirt
in the cup

what do you have?/ amulet

a drawer full of fishnets with their crotches ripped out
from strong legs that never learned or liked to cross themselves
like a lady
a loud voice that can bray, sound like a white lady on the phone
and whisper honey comfort
the ability to ask for lower credit terms and extensions
the ability to do yoga at terminal B or a truck pullout
the rolodex of resources in my brain
the pebble from a tiny redwoodcreek we did ceremony at
cut pieces of our hair for the river and burnt sweet black sage
smoke
before we gathered nettles for the year's veins
tucked in the pocket of my forever21 heart purse to remember
you by
two passports
two names
ancestors who gave me pretty feet
with high arches and hard hard soles
to walk long distances

the ability to work a value village
the ability to work a tj maxxx
the ability to throw a clothing swap
the ability to not feel shame for not being able
to do something
the ability
to ask

a voice that can fill a room
a belly always hungry and filled

mason jars filled with water, honey and smoke

your text message folded into a locket banging on my sternum heart:
knock 'em dead crip star. don't let the bastards get you down. you'll be in my heart tonight and long after.

you know I'm gonna

one day i'll give birth to a tiny baby girl
and when she's born she'll scream and I'll tell her to never stop
—Nicole Blackman

I want to raise her on oakland
on the lift of her mama's eyebrow
on gilded mornings bodega walk and stoop sitting intelligence
on the global brown collective
intelligence of our aunty tribe
of curly hair loved with conditioner.

you know i'm gonna raise her
on curls combed out gentle, always while wet
on the finger held up, an arched eyebrow,
her mama's crooked smile. on hip shift walks.
I'm gonna give her the richness I didn't have:
of a stoop. of a big noisy kitchen table, of being rocked by many hands
at the meeting and the show. of you can sleep in a desk drawer,
us second generation mixed girls make sure to give our kids
the vastness of enough tubs of neon yellow shea butter
and coconut oil gone liquid on the shelf,
a million hot pink gold leopard knock-off rocawear kicks bought off ebay.
you know I'm gonna raise her to know how to smile
and give good cut eye, rock the library
and then go explode the whole known world
which is like explore but with just one letter different
you know.

nice brown parents

gesig's dad drove fifteen hours to see her
brought us 20 crabs and some lobster
fixed the internet
called her little girl in mi'kmaq
and asked if she wanted to go to costco

gabe's mom lived in the basement with him for a couple months
made all us qpoc roommates cucumber salad
lovingly talked shit and chucked him upside the head
let him borrow the car to take me to the airport

me and my friends
we just stare
at the nice brown parents
we still don't have

my friends' babies
laugh and fall over
freak out and get held
no one is screaming
there is a purple house
all of us singing songs and pushing the stroller
to get shwarma for lunch

I sink into
the vast calm quiet
of the after
the nice brown parent
I didn't have
the sweet salt release
from my face

the day I decided to have you

dear one: the day I decided to have
you, I was scared shitless. Gaza was burning.
Four children who looked just like you were bombed to death
for wanting to touch water.
Oakland was drought as parable of the sower.
When my mother had me, she didn't know if we'd have a next nuclear winter
Your dad told me our Lankan staying chant, and I blurted out my ask
on the steps of the Tamil coop. He said yes. Mary Lambert was playing
on the value village sound system and I was one long shriek of emotion.
I was scared shitless. but we had our long story of improbable survival and joy,
and I, I had you.

the worst thing in the world

this is the truth: every worst thing you can imagine will come true. you and your ex bff will be asked to keynote a conference together, and both of you will say yes.
your daughter will indeed hate you. mothering and living are both losing propositions. that's
no reason not to do them. the answer is in what comes after. what you answered the worst thing in the world with. already in the afterfuture. breathe in breathe out. everything is not going to stop changing on you.

hey you sicksauce survivor stunner[1]
you who asked a lot will not always have the right answer.

we've always come on boats. we're going to keep coming. we know the waves and rough water.

bless the rough water and the small boats.
bless the worst thing.

---

1   *phrase by k. ulanday barrett*

Winner of the 2012 Lambda Literary Award, Leah Lakshmi Piepzna-Samarasinha is a queer disabled femme writer, teacher and performer of Burgher/Tamil Sri Lankan, Roma and Irish ascent. The author of *Love Cake* and *Consensual Genocide* and the co-editor of *The Revolution Starts At Home: Confronting Intimate Violence in Activist Communities*, her writing has been widely anthologized. She is the co-founder of the queer people of colour arts incubator Mangos With Chili, a lead artist with Sins Invalid and co-founder of Toronto's Asian Arts Freedom School. In 2010 she was named one of the Feminist Press' 40 Feminists Under 40 Shaping the Future. Her first memoir, *Dirty River*, is forthcoming from Arsenal Pulp Press in fall 2015.